AROUND DURSLEY
IN OLD PHOTOGRAPHS

AROUND DURSLEY
IN OLD PHOTOGRAPHS

COLLECTED BY
ANN WILSON & DAVID EVANS

ALAN SUTTON
1986

Alan Sutton Publishing Limited
Brunswick Road · Gloucester

First published 1986

Around Dursley in old photographs.
1. Cam (Gloucestershire)—Description—Views
2. Cam (Gloucestershire)—History
3. Dursley (Gloucestershire)—Description—Views
4. Dursley (Gloucestershire)—History
I. Wilson, Ann   II. Evans, David E.
942.4'19   DA690.C16/

ISBN 0 86299 311 3

Typesetting and origination by
Alan Sutton Publishing Limited.
Printed in Great Britain
by Redwood Burn Limited.

CONTENTS

CHARLES HOWARTH

*On 28 September 1986, and while
this book was being prepared for
publication, Charles Howarth of Uley
died, aged 82. 'Charlie' was not only
a superb photographer but to me a
great friend and I shall always
treasure the memories of my many
happy visits to him and his wife
Norah in their welcoming home. All
the pictures in this collection owe
much to his skill and the book is
therefore a tribute to a very
remarkable man.*

DAVID EVANS

INTRODUCTION

The first published volume of old photographs of Dursley and Cam created wide interest and we hope that this second volume, extended to include Slimbridge and other villages down to the banks of the river Severn, will do the same.

Many of the pictures are not dated simply because it is not known when they were taken. Most, however, must have come from the late Victorian and Edwardian period as this time was the great heyday of photography, amateurs and professionals recording everything that happened around them.

We are very grateful to all those people who so kindly lent us originals – their names are recorded at the back of the book. Many gave us information and we have tried to ensure that this is correct. However there are bound to be errors as human memory is fallable and most of us can make mistakes when recalling the past. If any are noticed, or if readers have extra information, we would be very happy to be contacted. Some pictures have names beneath them. In all cases, unless stated otherwise, these are recorded from left to right.

Three other people have our sincere appreciation. Charles Howarth of Uley, who has coaxed many a dead old picture back to life. Over very many years of association with us Charles must have printed several thousand pictures and has enabled us to build up our remarkable collection of photographs of this part of Gloucestershire. We are grateful too to Valerie Rodway who typed part of this text. We thank also our publisher, Alan Sutton, for his great interest and help in getting this collection into print.

Finally, we hope that all who see this book will enjoy being transported back into the past. If this happens, and if the occasional happy memory is rekindled, then this book will have served its purpose.

Ann Wilson,
9, The Close, Slimbridge
David Evans,
17, Kingshill Park, Dursley

SECTION ONE

Employment

RAYMOND HOLDER WITH BLOODWORTH'S BAKERY CART at the bottom of Crawley Hill, Uley.

DURSLEY'S POSTMEN — Back row: ——, ——, Frank Martin, Sam Brickhorn, Arthur Whittard, ——, ——, Fred Hitchins.
Front row: Tom Fussell, Frank Hadley, ——, ——, Jim Fussell. Telegraph boy Harry Trotman.

Earlier postmen wore a uniform of blue and scarlet and, when collecting mail for Dursley from Wotton-under-Edge or Cambridge, wore a sword as defence against highwaymen.

Right: R. A. LISTER & Co., RIVER'S MILL, C. 1903. What is now Mawdsleys was once Reeve's or River's Mill and by turns was used for paper making, wire drawing and wool cloth manufacturing. In the 1890s the mill began to make electric engines and in 1903 the premises were acquired by R. A. Lister & Co. This picture was taken about then. One of the engines shown here came to light recently and has been restored by Mawdsleys.

Below: STEAM ORGAN. In 1907 Listers sold River's Mill to H. St Hill Mawdsley of Taunton, and Mawdsley electric engines have long since had a world wide reputation. One speciality was the production of generators and motors for travelling showmen and there are still memories of their vehicles rolling into the company's premises in the 1920s to have these serviced.

Above: INSIDE ONE OF MAWDS-LEYS WORKSHOPS, c. 1910.

Left: CHAMPION & HALL, BOULTON LANE. Samuel Champion began making ropes and twines in 1778 and later began weaving cider and rick cloths. At the beginning of this century carpet production was added to the firm's operations which by then included the making of cocoanut matting, door mats, gym mats and rabbit nets. Mr J. Champion opened a factory for carpet making in Boulton Lane, Dursley, in 1910 and soon began producing seamless Axminsters and Anglo-Orient Reversibles. The building on the left was built in the 1890s as the headquarters of Elvey's brewery.

THE WOOL STORE AT BOULTON MILLS, c. 1920.

WEAVING RUGS AT BOULTON MILLS.

DURSLEY HIRING FAIR. The area has always been strongly rural. It was traditional for men and women wanting work to go to one of the hiring fairs held in local towns and this picture may be of such an occasion in Dursley.

THE CO-OPERATIVE SOCIETY, LONG STREET, DURSLEY. The Cainscross Co-operative Society was formed in 1863 and soon after it started to send goods to people in Cam and Dursley by train in a special hamper. Then followed a horse and cart service and finally, in 1891, the branch shop in Long Street was opened. The present shop, at the corner of May Lane, opened in 1910.

EZRA HARRIS outside his shop in Long Street, which was started by his father, Levi, in the 1860s when he was described as 'grocer, provisions dealer and butcher'. Ezra's mother can just been seen in the doorway, and on the right is one of his sons, aged about 7, who died not long after this picture was taken.

LONG STREET, DURSLEY. The men in the photograph are standing at the entrance to Champion's carpet factory, below which can be seen what was believed to have been a wool merchant's mansion of considerable age. On the right is Dursley Co-op.

CHAMPIONS RELIANCE WORKS WORKFORCE, 1880s. The gentleman in the front row with a beard is J. B. Champion, JP, owner of the firm and a leading figure in local society. The man wearing a top hat, second from the left behind the children, could be the chief clerk. Fourth from the right, back row, is a man with fibre round his waist. He is a rope maker about to produce yarn. This he would have done in a rope walk by walking backwards away from a wheel to which the yarn was attached. As he moved he pulled out fibres evenly and a boy turned the wheel to twist them. The yarns were then twisted in twos or threes to make twines and ropes.

WILLIAM HEWISH AND BILLY, THE HORSE, with other LMS railway carters about to take carpets from the Reliance Works to the station, c. 1910.

MEN AND BOYS RETURNING TO LISTERS AFTER LUNCHTIME, c. 1913.

LISTERS MACHINE SHOP, c. 1888. Robert Ashton Lister began his company in 1867, renting a water mill in Dursley to repair farm machinery, but soon afterwards he began making his own agricultural wares.

PEDERSEN'S BICYCLE WORKS. In about 1890, Mikael Pedersen, a Dane, came to Dursley with a design for a new style of bicycle. These were manufactured in Water Street for about fifteen years until the outbreak of World War I. In this photograph gears are being machined and many cycle frames hang in the background.

STEELE'S, PARSONAGE STREET, DURSLEY.

MR AND MRS STEELE in the garden at the back of the shop. Boots and shoes were made in the building on the right.

GEORGE NEALE who came from Somerset in the 1920s to make shoes for Steele's.

CYRIL CHANDLER, Steele's errand boy, in the mid-1920s.

CAM OR CORRIETT MILLS survived the collapse of the wool cloth trade in the 1840s and grew to a great size by World War I, as shown here. Though now much reduced in area, mechanization has meant that production is higher than ever. It is linked with Lodgemoor Mill in Stroud and the two mills produce cloth for tennis balls and Guards' uniforms. On the right the children wait on Cam railway station for a train.

CHARLIE FORD AND LEONARD AND LIONEL STEEL outside their bakery in Cam. The horses are Donnybrook Admiral and Dolly Grey.

A RURAL SCENE by Cam Pitch behind Whitehouse Farm in Chapel Street.

CARPENTERS THOUGHT TO BE FROM CAM MIDDLE MILLS. The boy in the front is holding a certificate so maybe they have just won a competition.

A 15 TON K-TYPE STEAM-ROLLER on the A38 near Gossington, c. 1917. The men seem to be having a lunch break – note the two gallon stone cider jars by the front roller. Frank Oakey, Norman Atwood, 'Cully' W. Palmer, Ruff the dog, G. Thornhill and George Palmer.

MISS N. EDWARDS OF WATEREND FARM first bred Coaley Fawn Ducks in 1901 specially for white egg production. The birds were described as a small breed, very alert and active. The basic colour was fawn but the drake had chocolate markings and the duck grey; bill and legs were orange. The breed was still in existence in 1927.

ARTHUR LACEY, GILBERT HURL, EDDIE MAY AND BERT PHILLIPS, in the doorway of Workman's Engineering Works, Slim-bridge. Workman's made waggons and carts, and around 1908 they developed a flat bed lorry, which had a full lock and could turn on it's own ground. They also made a cranked axle milk float. Mr Arthur Noad worked for the company for 49 years, and made all the patterns for castings used on the cider mills, for which Work-man's won great acclaim. They also serviced Centinal Lorries, renewing the steam pipes, and were the first to put rubber tyres on to their wheels.

PERCY BARTON OF NARLES FARM, CAMBRIDGE, Chairman of the Berkeley Heavy Horse Society formed in 1936. With him here, at about that time, is Mr W. Browning, groom, and the stallion Theale Camrose which was travelling the area.

SEYMOUR MERRET AT WHITEHALL FARM, CAMBRIDGE. Before moving here he farmed at Hornshill. One of his daughters married Lionel Steel of Cam Bakery.

DORIS CULLIMORE MILKING THE HOUSE COW STRAWBERRY, at New House Farm, Cambridge in early 1930s, a school holiday job when the men were hay-making.

BLACKSMITH WILLIAM BARTON shoeing a horse at Churchend Smithy, Slimbridge, c. 1884. In the house doorway are his wife and eldest children, Maud, Frank, Elsie and Fanny.

WILLIAM DANIELS making a cart wheel in his yard at Churchend. He served his wheelwright's apprenticeship at Workman's foundry.

ALBERT POWELL AND JACK FRYER with young Michael Hawkins of the Hurns Farm, Slimbridge at the corner of Longaston Lane.

Right: SHEPHERD BOWDITCH, left, was shepherd and shearer at New Grounds Farm, after moving to Slimbridge from Somerset in 1896. The shearing sheds were on the site of what is now the hostel and kitchen of the Wildfowl Trust, and sheep would be driven from farms all around the district to be shorn by Mr Bowditch and his team. Sheep and fleece would be taken to Gloucester market by barge, and the sheep would be penned beside the canal awaiting collection – hence the name, 'Shepherd's Patch'. Francis Bowditch is shown with Austin Pick, of Purton, who travelled the area as a slaughterer, and Frank Milsom, after dispatching a pig. *Below*: RECTORY FARM, SLIMBRIDGE, at the junction of Churchend and Troytown, one time home of Alice Haines, renowned for her cheeses. The cheese store was in the building on the right behind the house, now demolished. In the upper right corner can be seen The Hurns Farm. 'Hurns' means nook or bend.

CERTIFICATES AND AWARDS GIVEN TO ALICE HAINES with examples of the cheeses.

ALICE HAINES with a Shire Horse foal bred at Rectory Farm.

BAKER'S ROUNDSMAN, JACK GOODRICH, outside 'Major' Pearce's bakery, Churchend. The horse, Polly, belonged to Hartley Tudor, Mr Pearce's horse having died 'through being kept too near the ovens'. Mr Tudor helped Jack on the round by driving the van. On one occasion they stopped at several pubs on the way and Mr Tudor found he had sold his horse to Mr Pearce by the time he reached home! Jack went on to work for Steel's Bakery in Cam.

ROLLS COURT FARM, CAMBRIDGE, at haymaking time. Sam Brown, Bill Peake on the Deering grass cutter, and Frank Peake.

WILLIAM HUNTLEY, AND FRED AND BERT WYTCHARD harvesting at Cambridge House Farm, in 1917. The Wytchards lived at Rectory Farm Cottages.

THRESHING AT CAMBRIDGE HOUSE FARM, 1917. The machine belonged to Frank Exell of Cam who travelled with it round farms in the area. In the photograph are Joey Day, a carter; Sam Brown who did odd jobs; Frank 'Dummy' Phillimore who was deaf and dumb; Jonah Smith; and Walt Townsend the 'driver'. The soldier was Jack Cook of Thornbury who had been seconded to help with the harvest as World War I came to an end. He was billeted at the farm. On the thresher ready to feed in corn is Fred Hurd.

PLOUGHING AT CAMBRIDGE HOUSE FARM.

THE CAMBRIDGE ARM OF THE GLOUCESTER – SHARPNESS CANAL. The stretch from the main canal to what became known as Hudsons Wharf was opened in 1820, and plans were made to continue the branch through Cam and Dursley to Uley. The lady is probably Mrs Lewis Jones wife of a baker who lived by the wharf. The big building on the right was a warehouse and donkey stables.

SHARPNESS OLD DOCKS, opened 1827. The present docks were opened in 1874.

MOVING TIMBER BY HAND in Sharpness Docks, c. 1907.

CHANGING A GATE AT SHARPNESS DOCKS ENTRANCE, World War II. The operation could only take place at high tide and when the river was very calm. A new bearing for the gate can be seen centre. H. Nash, C. Savage, E. Chandler, D. Fowler, B. Deacon (passing funnel), O. Powell (carrying bearing), J. Lane.

CANAL MAINTENANCE WORKMEN ON THEIR WORK BARGE, c. 1920. On the roof of the house boat are Bill Deacon, holding the dog, B. Mortimore, G. Drinkwater, M. Malone and P. Brint. Standing: D. Hillman, W. Prosser, J. Markey, J. Wright, and F. Workman. Seated in the foreground: C. Cox, C. Day, H. Wilks, T. Cook, A. Rudge, J. Fildes, B. Woodward, E. Theyers, B. Smart and F. Field. The name of the boy is not known.

A MANGOLD HARVEST. The canal bank between Patch Bridge and Purton was used by Percy Barton to grow mangolds in the sludge dumped after dredging operations. The ground was unable to take carts and so the roots were taken by barge to the bridge where they were stored. Centre here is Edward Theyers, employed by Mr Barton. The Patch Bridge at the time was in two parts, each half being moved by a pole. Repairs were carried out by Joe and George Gabb who would cycle up from Saul with a portable forge and other tools.

A TUG PULLING A BARGE UP THE CANAL towards Gloucester, past the Berkeley Arms Inn at Purton.

TWO BARGES LOADED WITH WOOD, destined for Bryant and May's match factory in Gloucester, being towed past the Patch Bridge, Slimbridge.

Right: LONGBOAT, MOORED ON THE CANAL AT SHEPHERD'S PATCH. This was used by Peter Scott as accommodation for visitors to the Wild Fowl Trust, before the hostel was built. On the right can be seen a wharfage shed, built by Workman's Engineering Company in Slimbridge. It was used by Workman's of Draycott Mill for the storing of grain, and during World War I munitions were stored there. These were brought in mainly by a railway laid across the fields from the main line at Berkeley Road.

A GANG WORKING ON A CANAL-SIDE DITCH OR 'RHINE', dug to a depth of 14 feet.

MEN DEEPING BALDWINS BROOK, WHITMINSTER, again to a depth of 14 feet. To quote Bill Deacon, back row centre with dog, 'You had to be fit to throw shovels of wet mud fourteen feet into the air for twelve hours a day'. Note the two cider flagons in use!

A STURGEON CAUGHT IN A SEVERN PUTCHER — a cone shaped basket set up on the river bed at low tide. Sturgeon have to be offered to the Queen though not all are accepted. In the mid 1940s, though, one was taken to Buckingham Palace by Mr Baldwin of Berkeley and his son.

THE WORKHOUSE, seen here high above Dursley, was built in the 1830s to replace more liberal parish work-houses in the area. Conditions were harsh and the stigma and shame at going in was immense.

By the 1920s conditions had changed for the better. This picture shows two charabancs of people from Dursley Poor Law Institution, as the workhouse was then called, with Officers and Guardians of the Poor, about to set off on their annual outing in July 1927.

High Days & Leisure Time

A HUNT MEETING at the turnpike crossroads, Uley, c. 1916.

MAYPOLE DANCING at the Uley Sports, 1903.

OPENING THE NEW DURSLEY WATERWORKS on the Caswell stream beyond Highfields. Centre, presumably with a glass of water each, are Messrs Harrold, Prout, Close and Ford.

DURSLEY FIRE BRIGADE outside its headquarters in Bull Pitch, c. 1905, decorated for a festive occasion.

GIRLS OF MISS GARRETT'S DANCING SCHOOL entertain workhouse inmates, c. 1936. Master of the institution, Mr Wilson, stands second from the right.

THE INTERIOR OF THE VICTORIA CINEMA, SILVER STREET, DURSLEY. Opened in the 1880s as a Temperance Hall, it was later used as a venue for concert parties before becoming a cinema in the days of silent films. It is now the Victoria Market.

THE OLD BELLS OF ST JAMES'S CHURCH, DURSLEY. In 1904 it was discovered that the framework holding these was in a dangerous state and that the bells themselves were in a poor condition. They were taken down and a new peal hung the following year. In March 1906 a new clock and carillon were installed.

THE NEW BELLS ABOUT TO BE HUNG in 1905.

DURSLEY CHURCH LADS BRIGADE, in blue uniforms, marching through the Market Place to the monthly church parade. The C.L.B. was attached to St James's Church.

DURSLEY C.L.B. SOCCER TEAM, 1913–14, for three years unbeaten in their league. Captain Walters, left, and Lieutenant Bert Chandler, right, were brigade officers. Second from left, middle row, is Cyril Smith and centre front row is C. Preater. Both later played for the Dursley Rovers team.

THE C.L.B. ANNUAL CAMP, 1912. In this year it was at Dawlish, where high winds blew down many tents.

THE C.L.B. CAMP AT WEST BAY, BRIDPORT, 1913. A home-made wireless station was built that was capable of receiving transmissions from the Eiffel Tower in Paris. Many of the boys had fathers who belonged to the Volunteer Rifle Brigade, and the boys themselves became proficient in the use of a rifle. Older members were among the first to enlist and go to France at the beginning of World War I.

DURSLEY GAS COMPANY'S CENTENARY DINNER in Listers Hall, 1936. Centre, top table, is Sir Percy Lister, director. On his left is Francis Bloodworth, managing director.

VISIT OF THE DUKE OF YORK, LATER KING GEORGE VI, TO LISTERS, December 1931. Here he is seen leaving the Priory, Long Street. The Duke was president of the Industrial Welfare Society which aimed to improve the knowledge of public school boys, often the managers of the future, and working class lads, often already wage earners. Listers played a prominent part in the Society and so became very well known to the Duke.

A PEACE PAGEANT ON THE LAWNS OF THE PRIORY, 1919. The theme of the pageant was 'Dursley through the ages' and this group are druids and ancient Britons!

THE 1ST DURSLEY SCOUT TROOP, 1915. The troop had begun at the Tabernacle Congregational Church in 1908 and so was one of the first to be formed in the country. At the back are Bruce Champion, Scoutmaster, and W.S. Whittard, assistant. Back row: W. Chandler, S. Cross, ?, W. French, R. Hewish, V. Harris, A. Parsons, E. Game, V. Barnett, B. Griffin, H. Tocknell. Middle row: C. Whittard, I. Harris, W. Barnett, A. Webb, T. Rudge, A. Powell, T. Lockier, I. Letcher. Front row: I. Tocknell, P. Hancock, A. Wood, H. Wood, S. Hancock. The picture was taken at the troop headquarters, Prospect Place School.

SIR ASHTON LISTER OPENS A NEW BOWLING GREEN on the recreation ground, Dursley, May 1920.

A FESTIVE PROCESSION MOVES ALONG PARSONAGE STREET TOWARDS DURSLEY MARKET PLACE. To the left of the picture are two identical three storey buildings. The first was Smiths, the chemist, predecessor of Boots; the second, Bailey's newsagents shop. On the extreme right is the town's main post office, its position proclaimed by the lettering on the gas lamp in front of it.

AN ENTRY IN THE PROCESSION.

MAYPOLE DANCING ON DURSLEY'S RECREATION GROUND in 1910 to celebrate the coronation of George V. Ivy Owen, Evelyn and Norah Harrold, Irene Richards, May Workman, Lily Whittard, Lucretia Trollope, Doris Dimery, Miriam Whittard, Violet Hill, Dolly Chester and ? Mahoney.

R.E. HARROLD, JP LAYS THE FIRST BRICK ON THE WATTS ESTATE, KINGSHILL, April 1936 – probably now part of a house in Jubilee Road.

MRS GRACE MURRAY AND HER BROWNIE PACK, C. 1948. On the left is guide Heather Young who took over the pack when Mrs Murray had to retire through ill health.

DURSLEY D.S. & S. SOCCER CLUB COMMITTEE AND PLAYERS, 1919–20.

DURSLEY RUGBY FOOTBALL CLUB, 1898–9.

DURSLEY GYMNASTS.

A PIGEON LOFT ABOVE FORTFIELDS. Second from the left is Alfred Cross.

THE 'KNUT'S CLUB' which met at the Cross Keys Inn, Boulton Lane, Dursley. Two of the men have runner beans hanging from their top pockets. Cabbages are growing in front of them.

DURSLEY BICYCLE CLUB, 1907. Three of the cycles have oil lamps; the fourth carries a much more expensive acetylene lamp.

STINCHCOMBE BAND outside St Cyr's Church.

FLOWER SHOW AND SPORTS DAY AT STINCHCOMBE MANOR in the days of Lady Provost.

CAM CHORAL SOCIETY, c. 1930. Seated behind the table in black is Mrs Thomas, wife of Frederick, headmaster of Hopton School for many years. On her right is Vera Taylor, also a well known schoolteacher. Percy Ashworth stands in the back row second from the right.

PREPARING FOR A CARNIVAL. The John Bull figure is Lionel 'Jolly' Steel of Cam bakery.

A CROWD GATHERED AT THE JUBILEE TREE, CAM, to watch a band play its way up the High Street.

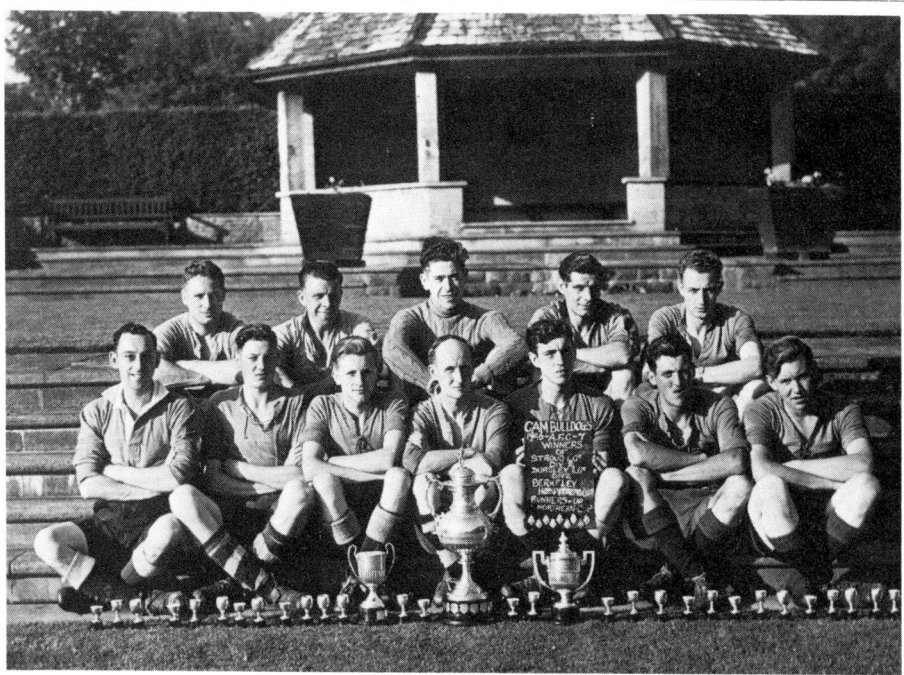

CAM BULLDOGS SOCCER TEAM, 1946–7, in the grounds of the former Winterbotham Memorial Gardens near the Railway Inn, Cam. The team were winners of the Stroud and Dursley Leagues, Berkeley Hospital Cup and runners-up in the Northern Cup that season.

CAM HARRIERS, C. 1931.

CAM MILLS SOCCER TEAM PLAYING AT THE MILL. Third from right is Jack Taylor.

Cam Mills' tribute to the Memory of the

Kingswood Football Team

Victims of a "Football Disaster" at Sharpness
on April 22nd, 1905

In spite of the Kingswood "poet's" gush
His promised "reception" and warning;"
Cam Mills "knocked out" the Kingswood team
And now for the MEDALS there's MOURNING.

No one knows how much they miss them.
None but Kingswood hearts can tell
How they miss those Silver Medals
Cam Mills hath done this thing well.

"How have the mighty fallen."

AN 'IN MEMORIUM' CARD printed by the Cam Mills team.

GIRLS FROM CAM MILLS MENDING SHOP (where flaws in the woven cloth were repaired) about to set off on a picnic. The two boys are Frank Malpass and Alec Taylor.

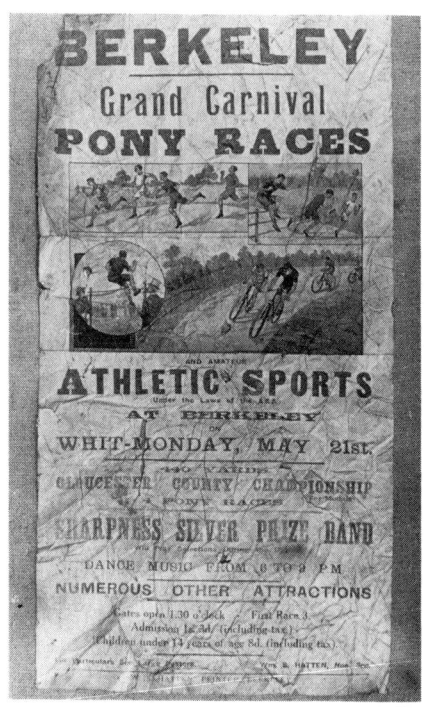

BERKELEY SPORTS, c. 1905.

THE SLIMBRIDGE FLOWER AND HORSE SHOW at Narles Farm, Cambridge, c. 1924. Group on the left: Francis Daniels of Middle Mill Farm, Stone, J. Daniels on the pony and Bob Cox of Moorend Farm. Centre group: Gilbert Clutterbuck of Lugs Farm, Sharpness, B. Collard of The Patch, ?, Evan Hill of Whitehouse Farm, Cambridge. Right hand group: G. Morgan, Churchend Farm, Slimbridge, J. Smith of Camplepit Court, Slimbridge, William Haines of The Hurns.

PRINCESS ELIZABETH MEETING SOME SLIMBRIDGE VILLAGERS during her visit to the Wild Fowl Trust, 1948. On her left is Peter Scott. Later the princess went to see a gypsy caravan, which had been renovated, in a field at the Tudor Arms Inn. Amongst the onlookers are J. King, Mrs Morris, Mrs Ted Hill, Rose Timbrell, Mrs Pegler and her children, Mrs Daniels, Marjorie Timbrell and her daughter, Myrtle, and Mrs George Jones of Breadstone.

EASTINGTON VOLUNTEER BAND at the fête held on the Longlands, Cambridge, May 1902.

SLIMBRIDGE A.F.C. 1922–23. Back row: ?, A.E. Tudor, ?, Charlie Day holding a child. Middle row: W. Pegler, J. Milsom, George Medcroft, Reg Hillier, Daniel Smith, Bert Theyers. Front: D. Moss, Redvers Dimery, ?, W. Day, Albert Webb, Harry Medcroft.

SLIMBRIDGE CRICKET CLUB, 1913. Back: ?, ?, W. Daniels who was lodging at Khetland, Moorend and apprenticed as wheelwright and carpenter at Workmans; Fred Cole of Bristol Road, Pedersen cycle fitter; Hubert Cuff of Whitney Cottage, Ryalls Lane, saddler; Lewis Jones of Cambridge, baker. Front: Fred Hawkins of Hill House, Cambridge, farmer; Harry Cuff, of Churchend, Slimbridge, a churn maker at Listers; Billy Burnett of Hurst Farm, Moorend, son of a farmer; Constable W. White of the police station, Cambridge, team captain; Stanley Morgan of Churchend Farm, Slimbridge, trainee auctioneer; Ted Theyers of Churchend, canal bank maintenance man.

SLIMBRIDGE FISHING CLUB, 1920s. Mr Percy Barton is seen standing far right with the gun which was used to start and close competitions. He rented the canal bank from the Patch to Purton. Other men in the picture include Bert Smith, Ewart Young, Harry White (centre back), Edgar Pegler, Harry Workman and Bill Pegler.

PREPARING FOR THE BICYCLE RACE, Slimbridge sports day, 1921. The cyclist on the left is Charlie Day.

SLIMBRIDGE SPORTS DAY, 1920, held on the Longlands behind the White Lion Inn, Cambridge. The field was owned by Harry Peake of Rolls Court Farm. In this picture of the start of the donkey race are W. Peake, W. Harmer, H. White, P. Barton, T. Young, Harry Perrett on a donkey, P.C. Robert Marsh, Harold Davies on a donkey, Charlie Day on a donkey, Joe Smith, J. Young, W. Hobbs and his son on a donkey.

SHARPNESS PLEASURE GROUNDS by the River Severn, between the old and new docks. A band is playing far right. The grounds were a great attraction for many years.

PADDLING IN THE MURKY WATERS OF THE RIVER SEVERN by the Sharpness Pleasure Grounds. In the background is the jetty marking the entrance to the new docks.

Church, Chapel and School

WOODMANCOTE AGRICULTURAL AND COMMERCIAL GRAMMAR, DURSLEY, c. 1878. The school opened in 1840 as a fee-paying boarding school and provided a good education for boys for over 60 years. Second from right, back row, is probably William Want, headmaster 1850 – 1888, described as 'a fine schoolmaster of the old fashioned type who believed in a thorough grounding in the three Rs'. He was Bailiff of Dursley 1857–8.

COTSWOLD HOUSE SCHOOL, WOODMANCOTE, c. 1890. It was run at this time by Miss Augusta Cott, probably centre here, sitting sideways. The standard of education at the school was very good and several went straight into university – a rare occurrence at the time. Like many girls' schools, boys were taught here until they reached the 'age of reason'. Later the school was taken over by Mrs Wintle and transferred to purpose built premises in Long Street, keeping the name of Cotswold House.

WATER STREET CHAPEL-CUM-SCHOOL, DURSLEY, built by Cam Meeting Presbyterian minister, Joseph Twemlow in 1718. It was used as a meeting house for worship on Sundays until about 1800 and as a charity school for the children of 'Protestant Dissenters' during the week. It closed in the late 1800s but its endowments remain in trust and are used to provide bursaries for non-conformist students.

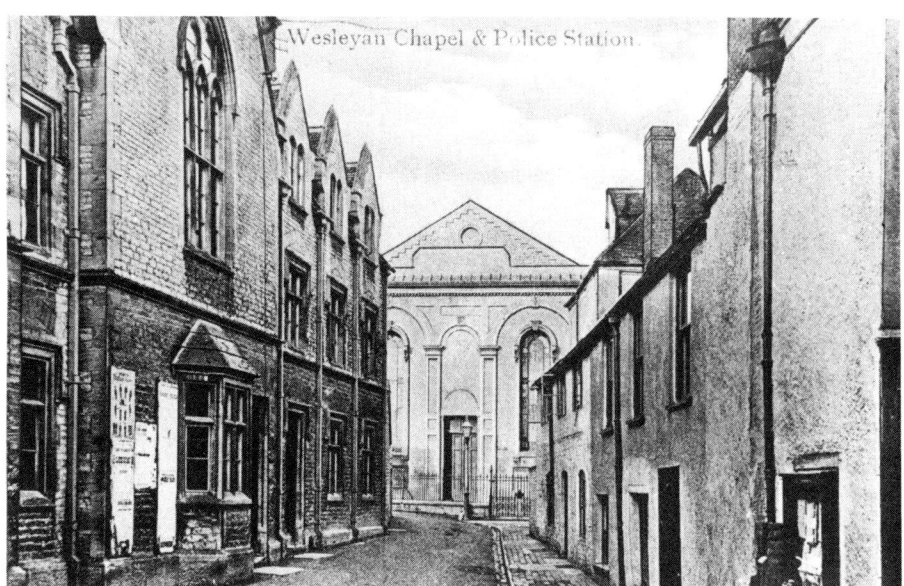

DURSLEY METHODIST CHAPEL, c. 1900. The roadway was then part of The Knapp. On the left are the police station and court house.

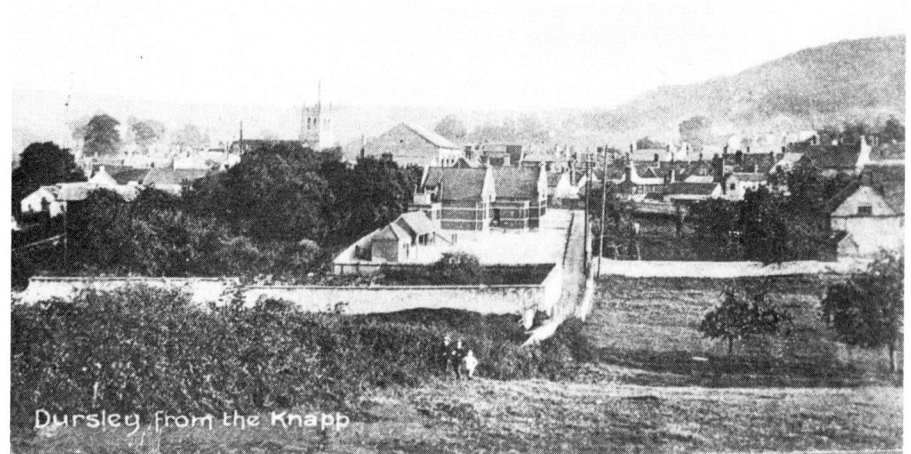

THE KNAPP, a narrow path starting at the Rednock estate, Dursley, can be seen here winding its way past the Methodist 'Victoria School' to the Market Place. The school was built to commemorate the diamond jubilee of Queen Victoria and replaced buildings in Boulton Lane. On the right is Castle Farm.

PARSONAGE PLACE PREPARATORY SCHOOL, DURSLEY, c. 1929, run by Miss Watts, standing right, mainly as a school for the children of tradesmen. The one schoolroom was upstairs and here Miss Watts was very keen on good conduct and self discipline. Back: Audrey Rose, May Squires, Mary Booy, Vera Blunsden, Margaret Blunsden. Third row: Jessie Everall, Mary Hitchins, Betty Townsend, Joan Kingham, Audrey Hemmings, Mary Blunsden. Second row: Rex Wise, Joan Whinfrey, Tommy Blunsden, Betty Kingham, Lilian Everall, Dorothy Thould. Front: ? , Ruby Butcher, John Jenkins, Bobby Field, Mary Hope.

DURSLEY RECTORY, 1866, now 100 Kingshill Road. It is possible that in pre-Reformation times the building was a small monastery-type hostelry for the use of travellers and incorporated a chapel. In 1563 it was called the Parsonage and was in a ruinous state. In 1719 a commission was sent to look at it and recommended that parts be demolished, and the remainder repaired or rebuilt. This was done and the resulting smaller building may have been as seen here. In the 1860s rector Canon Madan built a new rectory nearby and in about 1870 he knocked down much of the old rectory and used what was left to house a servant.

PUPILS OF DURSLEY SECONDARY SCHOOL dressed for a performance of *The Pirates of Penzance*, 1925. The school was founded in 1921 and later became a grammar school.

THE SECONDARY SCHOOL SPORTS DAY, c. 1925.

HEADMASTER FREDERICK THOMAS AND HIS WIFE outside Hopton School, Cam, founded in the early eighteenth century.

A CRICKET MATCH ON THE GREEN OUTSIDE HOPTON SCHOOL. The whole school seems to be present.

MERVYN BUSTON, sometime farmer at Woodmancote and founder of Dursley's Timber Turneries (extreme right), with his car outside Cam Methodist Chapel. It is about to be used to ferry performers of a missionary play out to country churches in the same circuit. Fourth from left is Revd Boggis. Sitting on the running board is Vera Taylor, then and for several years a pupil teacher at Upper Cam National School for girls.

THE ONLY DAME SCHOOL IN CAM, run by the two Miss Packers in a cottage in the middle of Chapel Street in the 1880s.

THE MANSE OF UPPER CAM CONGREGATIONAL CHAPEL (CAM MEETING). Revd Owen Griffiths is standing outside. The manse was at the bottom of Cam Pitch, and was later converted to a Co-op store.

ST JOHN'S CHURCH, SLIMBRIDGE, C. 1912. At this time the spire was strengthened and the bells removed, three to be tuned and two to be recast. A sixth was added and all were hung on a new steel frame. The top 15ft of the spire was rebuilt as the capstone had split.

CHURCH ARMY SISTERS visit Slimbridge Church in 1932 while on a zig-zag walk from Gloucester to Weston-super-Mare to hold a seaside 'sands mission'. They held a service for women and later for all parishioners before going on their way.

SLIMBRIDGE SCHOOL, opened in 1906 by R.A. Lister at a cost of 'a trifle over £9 per pupil'. There were three classrooms, designed to hold a total of 200 pupils. Mr Ellis, headmaster, is on the right of the left-hand door.

SLIMBRIDGE SCHOOL GARDEN. Each boy had a plot to cultivate, and in the early 1920s the boys gardened, while the girls were taught to sew. Later the headmaster's house was built on much of this land.

PURTON SCHOOL, built in 1874 by Muller Homes of Bristol, accommodated both day and Sunday schools. It was closed in 1930, demolished, and four garages built on the site. The cottage with the horse and cart outside used to be the police station, and backs onto the canal.

ST ANDREW'S CHURCH, SHARPNESS. The Bible and lectern were given by the congregation of Owlpen Church.

THE BRISTOL ROAD OUT OF CAMBRIDGE, showing the Congregational church, now demolished.

CAMBRIDGE CONGREGATIONAL CHURCH, opened in 1920, replacing an earlier building erected 1807. There was a schoolroom through the door to the right where Mr and Mrs Eves of the village shop taught the children on Sundays. The chapel became a Kingdom Hall for Jehovah's Witnesses before being demolished in 1982.

CAMBRIDGE, looking south. The village school (left), was built in 1862 with accomodation for 60 children. The Bell Inn (extreme right) was once also used as an auction room and as a 'Crowner's (coroner's) Court'. One inquest was into the death of a Cambridge lady found burned to death on her hearth. The building adjoining the inn belonged to it and contained outhouses, and wash house. Mr Payne with the bicycle worked at Cam Mills.

DAVID MOSS B.A. and his pupils at Cambridge village school. Mr Moss was headmaster for 32 years and at his funeral his assistants, Miss Davies, seen here on his right, and Emma Riddings, daughter of the Rector of Slimbridge, lined his grave with moss and primroses. His obituary said 'his loss is a public calamity'. As a memorial to him, pupils and parents placed a window depicting the Good Shepherd in Slimbridge parish church.

SECTION FOUR

Transport

THE BELL AND CASTLE HOTEL, Parsonage Street, Dursley. The sign advertises the hotel as having 'livery, posting and bait stables'. Tom Vigus was proprietor at this time. The carriage probably belonged to the hotel and was available for hire.

EVE'S BAKERY, CAMBRIDGE, served teas and, as the board over the door records, it was a 'Cyclists' Rest'. Eve's were renowned for their cakes and bread, and deliveries were made around the district by pony and trap.

CAMBRIDGE TURNPIKE HOUSE used to stand on the rise at the end of Elmcote Lane. In this picture, taken about 1935, are Harold Davies, his wife, and son Michael. Early deeds describe the building as having a 'kitching, back kitching, cellar and pantry' on the ground floor, and two bedrooms on the 'chamber floor'. It was demolished in the 1950s when the A38 was widened.

A REMOVAL SERVICE, 1913. Mervyn Buston, the owner, later began Timber Turneries in May Lane, Dursley.

WILLIAM BAKER, *coffin maker* of Cambridge, and his wife and child. On the running-board is a petrol can and the vehicle sports acetylene headlamps.

HARRY CUFF, a churn maker at Listers, with his son Arthur, at Churchend, Slimbridge, c. 1926.

EVE'S DELIVERY VAN, CAMBRIDGE. The shop's popularity continued into the motor age and lorry drivers often called in for cups of tea and a cake. Children preferred to buy their sweets from Mrs Eve as she was generous – Mr Eve was much more careful when weighing out!

A VIEW OF CAMBRIDGE FROM THE DURSLEY ROAD. A Dursley-bound bus is standing at the entrance to Cambridge Mill and a Centinel lorry is turning in from the Bristol direction, going perhaps to Workmans in Cam.

A GLOUCESTER BUS AT CAMBRIDGE, C. 1930. Mary Davies is standing in the doorway of the post office. The wall is hung with chocolate machines and to the right of the door is a bus timetable.

CAMBRIDGE, SHOWING THE RAC BOX, in front of which the patrolman seems to be saluting. Near the signpost there was a gap in the railings to allow cattle and horses to drink at the brook. On the other side of the road can be seen the conifer planted in 1897 to celebrate Queen Victoria's Diamond Jubilee. It died in 1985 and has been cut down.

THE DURSLEY DONKEY. Opened as a private railway in 1856, it closed to passengers in 1962 and to goods traffic in 1968.

MIDLAND RAILWAY EMPLOYEES AT DURSLEY STATION. Mr Warren, station-master, is second from left in the front row. Behind him, second from right, is Henry 'Jack' Jackson, a railway guard.

THE RAILWAY SIDINGS OF R.A. LISTER & CO. LTD, showing how much the company depended on trains in the 1920s to shift its products and receive raw materials. The passenger line to Dursley runs left to right between the hut (centre foreground) and the train.

THE LAST PASSENGER TRAIN AT DURSLEY STATION, 8 September 1962. The engine, a 2–6–0 Ivatt class 2P, heading the last 'donkey', carries a bunch of carrots.

BOB HARRIS, carter for the LMS railway, with his horse.

A TRAIN FOR DURSLEY WAITS AT COALEY JUNCTION, c. 1961. An incident some years before is commemorated in the rhyme: The Dursley Donkey never brayed and never ran off the line, but once at Coaley junction it left its tail behind!

THE SIGNAL BOX AT COALEY JUNCTION, August 1962.

THE LAST FREIGHT TRAIN TO DURSLEY runs along by Everlands, 28 June 1968. The picture was taken from Gallows or Gallas Bridge.

A TRAIN AT SHARPNESS ABOUT TO CROSS THE SEVERN RAILWAY BRIDGE. Behind the tall warehouse are the new docks, and the wooded area top right marks the pleasure grounds at Sharpness Point.

THE SEVERN RAILWAY BRIDGE was opened in 1879, a great engineering achievement at the time. One foggy night in October 1960 two barges carrying oil up-river to Sharpness docks collided and, helpless, were carried into the bridge by the racing in-coming tide. Two spans were brought down. By 1970 the rest of the bridge had been removed.

THE *SEVERN KING*, one of the Aust Ferry boats, was used to help in the demolition of the Severn Bridge. On 4 July 1969 she broke adrift and became impaled on the stump of one of the bridge piers, as seen here. The loss of the bridge changed life in the area. Children from Purton who had gone to Lydney Grammar School now could not, and June Reynolds, then living in Lydney but teaching at Dursley Grammar School, was faced for several months with an arduous journey via Gloucester. Such problems were multiplied many times over.

STEAM PACKETS once ran a regular service along the Gloucester – Berkeley Canal, stopping at many points along the way. The whole journey took 2½ hours. Before the days of car travel, the two boats, the *Wave* and the *Lapwing*, were important links between canal-side communities. Here one of the boats is going north past Purton . . .

. . . and here one is moored in Sharpness Docks.

THE CONVICT SHIP AT SHARPNESS. In 1906 the barque *Success*, once used as a prison ship in Australia, toured the English coast as a floating exhibition. She had been fitted as a ship used to transport convicts some seventy or more years before. Some of the cells are shown here and several contained dummy prisoners. Also on show were leg irons, handcuffs, cat-o-nine-tails and other items. In such a ship the three Davies brothers of Dursley may have been transported to Tasmania in 1824 for stealing meat and a brass pot. George was 17, Edward 19, and John 21.

People

EDWIN EYRE, who in 1876 bought the Kingshill estate, Dursley, from T.W. Richards, maltster. In the same year he remodelled the exterior of the old gabled mansion to give it its present appearance. At the end of the work he entertained the workmen who had been employed on the job to tea and dinner at the Bell and Castle Inn. His mansion is now used by the Stroud District Council.

CAPTAIN G.A. GRAHAM bought the Oaklands estate, Dursley, in 1865 and changed its name to Rednock. He played a major part in rescuing from extinction, the Irish Wolf Hound as a breed, and in 1884 he founded the Irish Wolf Hound Society. He bred many of the animals at Rednock.

IRENE NORVILLE AND DURSLEY TABERNACLE SUNDAY SCHOOL CHILDREN, c. 1920. Miss Norville was a highly talented musician and a greatly loved person. On her right here is Elizabeth Phillips, née Brooks.

GEORGE LISTER, who, it is said, walked to Dursley from Yorkshire when a lad in about 1820. He was a man of great energy and to him can be traced what are now Dursley's two biggest companies, Listers and Mawdsleys.

SIR ASHTON LISTER, sometime M.P. and county counciller, son of George and founder of R.A. Lister & Co. Ltd., now Lister-Petter. He was a great benefactor to the community in many ways, not least in his efforts to get a county secondary school established in Dursley. He is seen here at the school's sports day soon after it opened in 1921. Beside him is the school's first, and greatly admired, headmaster Ernest Barrett.

THE WINTLE FAMILY at Cotswold House, Long Street, Dursley, c. 1911. Hilda, Grace, Winifred, Dolly, Richard, Ruby, Emily, Jess and Reginald. Richard and his brother had the well-known Wintle's shop in Long Street for many years, now The Lantern Café. Emily ran a school for young ladies, first in lower Woodmancote then in Long Street. Later her six daughters took charge, Grace being headmistress.

Left: ROBERT KINGSCOTE, master of the Dursley Union Workhouse for some thirty years from 1860. Before this he ran the Bull Inn, Woodmancote which gave Bull Pitch its name. *Right*: Hannah Daniels of Fortfields, Dursley, c. 1902, in the uniform of a midwife. She was not qualified but was greatly skilled and was much loved by the poorer people of the town, who were her main concern.

HENRY OR 'JACK' JOHNSON of Upper Woodmancote was a train guard who worked for a while from Dursley station. He was killed in a terrible crash at Charfield on 23 October 1928. A passenger express racing towards Bristol hit the tail end of a goods train moving late into a siding and then bounced into and ripped through a mail train running north to Gloucester. Gas cylinders in passenger coaches ignited and fire raged for 12 hours.

THE CHARFIELD CRASH, taken by a *Dursley Gazette* photographer.

Left: MIKAEL PEDERSEN and his wife, c. 1898. He came to Dursley in the wake of a deal with Listers to market his improved version of a cream separator, the Alexandra, a product that did much to give Listers its international reputation. With him, Pedersen brought the idea of a new style bicycle, seen here, triangulated and with a string hammock saddle. Mikael was a warm hearted, eccentric man, the originator of many useful and not so useful inventions. His magneto design was much used in aircraft during World War I. He came to England rich from his deal with Listers and returned to his native country at the end of World War I, pennyless. *Right*: ANDERS MELLERUP riding a Pedersen motor cycle, c. 1905. Cam Peak is in the background. Anders came from Denmark to join Mikael Pedersen in his cycle works. Later he became the first non-family director of the Lister company.

SIDNEY BLOODWORTH, builder, and his family at Claremont, Kingshill Road, Dursley. He was the last Bailiff of Dursley, national re-organisation of local government abolishing this office in 1886.

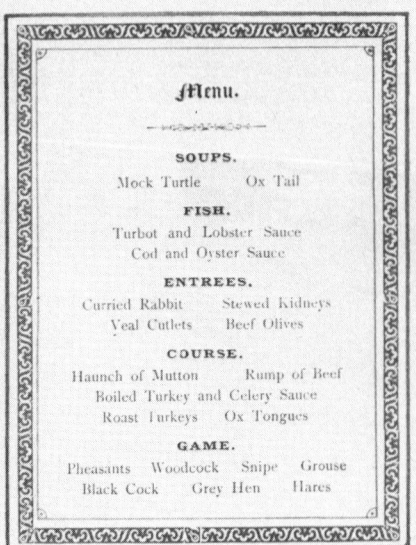

Menu.

SOUPS.

Mock Turtle   Ox Tail

FISH.

Turbot and Lobster Sauce
Cod and Oyster Sauce

ENTREES.

Curried Rabbit   Stewed Kidneys
Veal Cutlets   Beef Olives

COURSE.

Haunch of Mutton   Rump of Beef
Boiled Turkey and Celery Sauce
Roast Turkeys   Ox Tongues

GAME.

Pheasants   Woodcock   Snipe   Grouse
Black Cock   Grey Hen   Hares

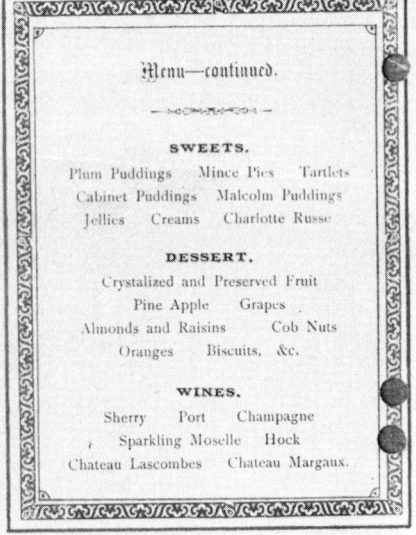

Menu—continued.

SWEETS.

Plum Puddings   Mince Pies   Tartlets
Cabinet Puddings   Malcolm Puddings
Jellies   Creams   Charlotte Russe

DESSERT.

Crystalized and Preserved Fruit
Pine Apple   Grapes
Almonds and Raisins   Cob Nuts
Oranges   Biscuits, &c.

WINES.

Sherry   Port   Champagne
Sparkling Moselle   Hock
Chateau Lascombes   Chateau Margaux.

THE MENU AT SIDNEY BLOODWORTH'S BAILIFFS' BANQUET 1885, held, as tradition demanded, on New Years Day.

FELIX LACEY AND HIS WIFE at Upthorpe Ironworks, well known for its repairs to farm machinery.

WILLIAM LACEY AND HIS FATHER, OLD JOHN. The Laceys were a well-known family in Cam, young John producing many of the photographs of the Edwardian era that have come down to us.

THE WEDDING OF WILLIAM WORKMAN, 1901. The picture was taken outside Primrose Cottage on the corner of Everside Lane, Cam, home of Granny Mitchel, seen here second from left. The bride is Granny Mitchel's youngest daughter. The Mitchel family was very poor – Granny had to bring up her own children and twin granddaughters, seen here in white. Her husband was too ill to work and she supported the family by selling salt, chitlings, faggots and sweets from her house. She also cleaned the infants' school by St Bartholomew's church. Mrs Winterbotham of Norman Hill House was interested in the family and ensured that the twins were kept well shod.

JOSEPH BALL, inn keeper of the Railway Inn, Cam, outside his hostelry with a dwarf, c. 1890.

JOSEPH BALL smartly dressed at the wedding of his daughter Amy to David Palser of Wotton-under-Edge. His wife Granny Ball is seated left and the picture was taken in the grounds of Cam Institute opposite the Railway Inn.

Above left: FANNY MANNING wheeling her milk along Green Street, Cam. She milked cows in the fields and trundled it home to Broomtree Cottage, next to Upthorpe Ironworks.

Left: MOURNING CARD. Cards such as these were very common in Victorian times.

Above right: WILLIAM HEWISH, c. 1900, coachman to the Winterbotham family of Norman Hill, Cam.

CANON THE REVD GEORGE MADAN came to the area in 1838 as Vicar of St George's Church, Upper Cam. He was a vigorous, energetic man who, having decided Lower Cam needed an Anglican church, set about providing one, drawing plans and acting as master builder. It opened in 1844 as St Bartholomew's. He left in 1852 to become vicar of St Mary Redcliffe in Bristol and here he undertook much restoration work. He also tried to modernize services and brought the wrath of many parishioners on his head. In 1865 he returned to become Rector of Dursley and here too found it difficult to change accustomed practices. His church of St James was very dilapitated and he had much of it rebuilt and enlarged. He also built a new rectory, now Dursley Court. He retired to Gloucester in 1887 and died a much loved man some 13 years later. His body was brought back to Dursley by train for the funeral.

WILLIAM HENRY WEBB, chimney sweep of Berkeley, with a wooden-wheeled 'bone-shaker' (left). William was first listed in county directories as sweep in 1897, by which time cycle design had progressed far beyond this type of machine. Nicknamed 'Spider', William was a common sight in the Berkeley area before and after World War I. He would ask children to look for the brush to appear through the top of a chimney and shout from inside the house 'Izzy foo!' This became the name by which local children knew him. He combined his job as sweep with the official position of town cryer, a post retained when he gave up chimney cleaning to become a bill poster around 1930.

FARMER JOHN SMART with his horse, Captain, c. 1890. John lived at Upper Upthorpe Farm and at one time weighed 21 stone.

A MYSTERY PICTURE found by a local builder in the chimney of an old house in Cam. The velocipede, or boneshaker, seems to be genuine, but does the photograph date from about 1870 when such machines were popular, or was it taken at a fancy dress event of a later date? And where was the picture taken?

GEORGE BOWDITCH, third son of Francis 'Shepherd' Bowditch. He, his brother William and Charles Nicholls risked their lives during the floods of 1910 at the New Grounds, Slimbridge, to rescue some 100 sheep from drowning. Later each man was presented with a heroism certificate by the Gloucestershire Society for the Prevention of Cruelty to Animals. George was a stockman at the New Grounds and died of TB when aged 34.

CHARLES NICHOLLS at a Berkeley Castle shoot when he was a loader. He was a gamekeeper at the Purton decoy pools, working for the Berkeley family. After one shoot at Slimbridge he and other men set off to walk back to Purton. One, Joe Pullen of Purton, fell into the canal and being unable to swim, Charles jumped in to help. Both men drowned.

WILLIAM (1807–1867) AND ELIZABETH (1814–1873) HILL, great grandparents of Ken Hall of Newlands Farm, Cam. The Hill family farmed for many years in the Gossington– Slimbridge area.

EDITH DAVIES OF CAMBRIDGE. Miss Davies was a certificated assistant teacher at Slimbridge Parochial and Cambridge village schools, moving to the new council school which amalgamated the two in 1906. She gave up teaching because of ill health and helped her aunt, Miss Mary Ann Davies, postmistress at Cambridge. On the death of her aunt in 1928 Edith took on the post. She was 101 at her death.

A picture of about 1930 of five folk then living within 20 yards of each other on the A38 at Cambridge, their combined ages being 402 years. Mr Estop, 85, still mowed and marked out the tennis courts behind the White Lion Inn; Mr. White, 84, builder, still climbed ladders; Mr. Payne, 80, worker at Cam Mills, was a keen and active gardener; Mrs Redding, widow of 77, had brought up a family of 8; Mrs Cole, 76, had raised 13 children.

War

THE GREY AND BLACK UNIFORM OF THE DURSLEY VOLUNTEER RIFLE BRIGADE IN ITS EARLY YEARS. The brigade was raised in 1861 and at first the uniform was free to volunteers; later it had to be bought, which effectively limited membership to the more prosperous traders. Shooting practice, using home-made bullets, was frequent on Stinchcombe Hill.

DURSLEY VOLUNTEERS AT A WEEK'S CAMP AT TEWKESBURY, July 1886, being by this time F Company 2nd Volunteer Battalion of the Gloucestershire Regiment. Notice the change of hat style to the glengarrie. Corporal Walter Bloodworth, with body pouch, stands left and Sergeant Wilkins sits right. The privates are F. Bloodworth, S. Osborne, J. Raggett, J.D. Shard and M. Timbrell.

VOLUNTEER ORDERS, as published in the *Dursley Gazette* in 1893.

DURSLEY VOLUNTEERS IN CAMP AT FARNBOROUGH, c. 1910. Reclining left is Mr Vigus.

THE CALL TO ARMS, 1914. Great crowds have gathered in Dursley Market Place to see volunteers off to war. People can be seen at most windows, including a maid at the top of what is now the National Westminster Bank.

LATER THE SAME DAY. The volunteers leave Dursley station by train.

WILLIAM WORKMAN of Shepherd's Patch, RSM in the Royal Field Artillery.

ASSEMBLING SHEEP SHEARS AT LISTERS. The rush of young men to join the army left factories and other businesses short of labour, and women filled the places.

MORE LISTER GIRLS. By estimate there are some 500 Lister girls in the bottom picture and a close study reveals faces of many ages. The fact that middle aged women, probably used only to domestic duties, got involved in engineering, indicated the strength of patriotism of the times. Sir Ashton Lister stands (back right); the group is assembled in the grounds of The Priory, Long Street, where now there is a bowling green.

WOVEN CARDS were a favourite means of communication from soldiers in France to families at home.

This plane could be a trainer from the aerodrome at Leighterton. It is a BE 2e built by the Royal Aircraft Factory at Farnborough and is probably fitted with a 95hp RAF 1A 8-cylinder engine which would have given it a top speed of 72mph.

AN R.E.8 AIRCRAFT with a top speed of 102mph, again built at Farborough, and powered by a 150hp RAF 4A 12-cylinder air cooled engine. The twin exhaust pipes project upwards from the cylinders at the front. This, too, may be a trainer from Leighterton and may have been photographed there, as some of the eight servicemen seem to be mechanics. Dated 7 August 1916, it is in one piece . . .

. . . which is more than can be said for this one which crash-landed behind the White Lion Inn, Cambridge, 11 July 1916.

Dursley,

Christmas, 1918.

The Townspeople of Dursley in asking your kind acceptance of the enclosed Christmas Present, wish to express their deep gratitude to all who are so nobly serving their Country at this ...

They join in praying for a speedy victorious Peace and your safe return ...

(Signed) S. BLOODWORTH, } Treasurers.
J. W. W. GIDDINGS, }
J. COLLETT, H.. Secretary.

The Treasury Note is sent owing to the great difficulty in obtaining suitable articles for the usual Christmas Parcel.

A GIFT CARD, 1918. Local servicemen received gifts at Christmastide from the town.

THE DEDICATION OF STINCHCOMBE MEMORIAL. With the end of the war came the reckoning in terms of human lives lost, and memorials sprang up all over the country.

THE DEDICATION OF THE SLIMBRIDGE MEMORIAL by the Revd Penny of Gloucester, standing in for the rector, Revd J.C. Carter, who was ill.

Dursley's memorial took the form of new gates to the Church of St James, an idea that provoked opposition from some of those whose religious allegiance was not Anglican. The dedication took place on 11 November 1922. Here soldiers march into the Market Place for the ceremony.

THE MEMORIAL GATES. The Union flag covering the gates has fallen away and the rector of Dursley, the Revd Dr C.C. Mills, by the pillar on the right, leads prayer.

WAR-WOUNDED AT ST MARTIN'S HOSPITAL, CHELTENHAM, 1922. Percy Hunt of Dursley, partially paralysed as a result of the war, is in the low chair in the centre. The occasion was a sale of work produced by these men and it was opened by Countess Bathhurst.

WORLD WAR II. Basil Woodward of Dursley was in France at the fall of Dunkirk. His unit was deployed to hold off the advance of the Germans as long as possible to allow the maximum number of soldiers to be evacuated. It meant that some in the unit had little chance of escaping and Basil was captured by the Germans. He is seen here at Ypres standing second from right with French soldiers and their German captors. After spending the duration of the war in a camp in Poland he returned to Dursley, the first POW home after fighting ceased. At the victory celebration he was one of those who lit the great bonfire on Stinchcombe Hill.

A PARADE OF CIVILIAN WAR DEFENCE ORGANISATIONS, held on Dursley's recreation ground, April 1940. Seen here talking with some of the firemen and ARP men is the Duchess of Beaufort.

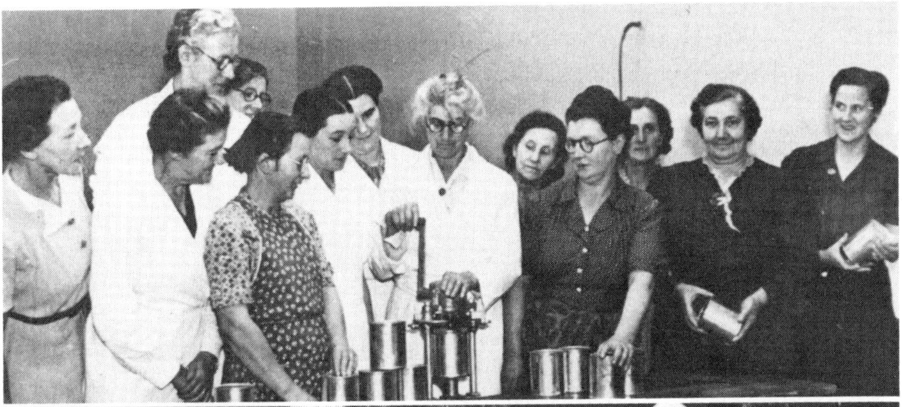

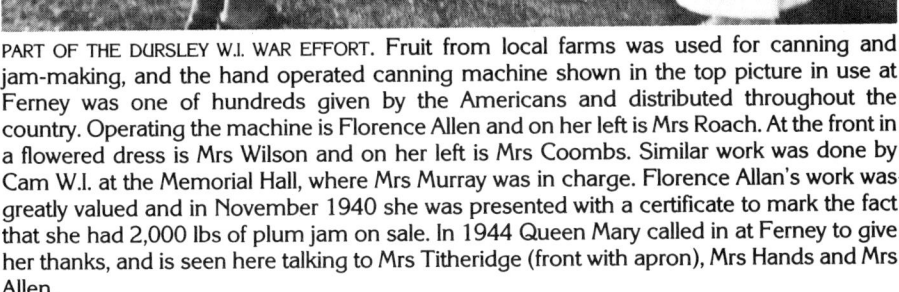

PART OF THE DURSLEY W.I. WAR EFFORT. Fruit from local farms was used for canning and jam-making, and the hand operated canning machine shown in the top picture in use at Ferney was one of hundreds given by the Americans and distributed throughout the country. Operating the machine is Florence Allen and on her left is Mrs Roach. At the front in a flowered dress is Mrs Wilson and on her left is Mrs Coombs. Similar work was done by Cam W.I. at the Memorial Hall, where Mrs Murray was in charge. Florence Allan's work was greatly valued and in November 1940 she was presented with a certificate to mark the fact that she had 2,000 lbs of plum jam on sale. In 1944 Queen Mary called in at Ferney to give her thanks, and is seen here talking to Mrs Titheridge (front with apron), Mrs Hands and Mrs Allen.

DURSLEY CIVIL DEFENCE VOLUNTEERS ON CAM LONG DOWN, c. 1940.

CAM NATIONAL FIRE SERVICE. At the beginning of the war each parish had its own fire fighting team, but later these small units were almagamated into bigger teams. The Slimbridge men joined those of Cam and used Cam Mills as a base. The section was manned every night, the men being paid 1s 6d (7½p) for an 8pm to 6am shift, out of which they were charged 1s for supper. They were called out by Lister's siren or by telephone. Two Slimbridge men can be identified here: Jack Moss, middle row, third from right; Ewart Daniels, back row, fourth from right.

'A.R.P. DURSLEY TEAM RESPIRATOR ASSEMBLERS, CHAMPION'. These folk at Champion's Reliance Carpet Works, Long Street, Dursley, assembled gas masks and boxes, all after their normal working hours.

BRIGADIER K. DUNN INSPECTING A PARADE OF THE HOME GUARD and making presentations on what is now Rednock School playing fields.

THE HOME GUARD marching down from Woodmancote, led by company commander Major E. Rae.

A MARCH-PAST IN KINGSHILL ROAD, DURSLEY. The saluting base is at the junction with 'Gas Works Pitch'.

DURSLEY CIVIL DEFENCE WARDENS parade up Kingshill Road in 1943.

QUEEN MARY VISITING MUNITIONS WORKERS AT LISTERS. She was a frequent visitor to this area, coming from Badminton House, and is seen here with Sir Percy Lister.

QUEEN MARY AT THE NEW GROUNDS, SLIMBRIDGE, on land which had been requisitioned for the 'Dig for Victory' campaign. The villagers were about to plant potatoes, sacks of which can be seen on the trailer in the background. Percy Barton and Percy Wherret, both parish councillors, are with her, along with members of the Berkeley estate and Ministry of Agriculture. The crop was eventually harvested by members of the local W.I.

For several years the Gloucester War Agricultural Committee organized harvest camps for children at the New Grounds, where now is the Wildfowl Trust. The camps were run by Reg Davis of Cam, who persuaded Queen Mary to visit one year. Here she is seen outside the first aid hut with the local Red Cross Commandant, Mrs Frank Lister, and two of the hut staff, Mrs Scott and Mrs Mary Smith.

CORPORAL WILLIS CHILDERS OF ARKENSAW was one of many American soldiers who stayed for a short while in Dursley. He is pictured here outside what was the the Regal Cinema in Kingshill Road.

END OF WAR CELEBRATIONS, held in Dursley Council School, now Dursley Technical College, 1945.

For some the horrors of war continued after fighting ceased. Michael Bailey of Bailey Newspapers Group was posted by the army to Japan and saw for himself in March 1946 the desolation wreaked by the Hiroshima bomb.

DURSLEY'S RECREATION GROUND was dedicated in 1951 as a memorial to the dead of World War II. This picture is believed to be of a happier event on the ground – a religious service on Coronation Day 1937, the robed figure being Philip Floyd of the Secondary School.

Places

OWLPEN MANOR dates back to the 1400s and seems to have changed little in the intervening years. Appearances, however, can be deceptive. By 1807 it was badly dilapidated and the position did not improve when some years later the owners abandoned it for a new Victorian mansion on the hill above – Owlpen House. The manor-house below was looked after by caretakers for some 100 years. In 1925 it was restored and new owners made it into a home again. Tradition has it that Margaret of Angou spent the night here before the battle of Tewkesbury in May 1471.

OWLPEN HOUSE was said to have been modelled on a London club. Most of the building was demolished in 1955 after a fire, and little now remains.

THE STREET, ULEY, C. 1900. The shop sign on the right advertises Elvey's Fine Ales and Stouts which would have been supplied from the brewery in Dursley.

THE LOWER END OF ULEY, C. 1900. On the right can be seen Uley turnpike house.

PART OF MARSH MILL, ULEY, C. 1900, near the turnpike. The mill proper was off the picture to the right at the end of the mill-pond. The slats at the upper window spaces of the big building allowed air to move through the top storey to dry wool or wool cloth hung there after dying. After the collapse of the wool cloth trade in the 1840s the mill became a sawmill.

THE RESTORED MILL WHEEL. During World War II Marsh Mill was occupied by the Bristol wood merchants, Scaddings. There was little for the men to do and some set about the restoration of the old mill wheel. This they got going in 'overshot' form and it remained on the site until about 1975.

UPPER WOODMANCOTE, c. 1908, with Mr Richards and family. His plant nursery covered a considerable area behind the house.

THE VIZARD ALMHOUSES, WOODMANCOTE, with St Mark's Church beyond. Both came into being through the generosity of Henry Vizard, the almhouses in 1853 and the church in 1844.

A VIEW FROM NEAR WOODMANCOTE MANOR, 1920s, across Rosebery Road to where the first houses are being erected on the Highfields estate.

QUEEN MARY BEING DRIVEN THROUGH WOODMANCOTE, 1922. The queen was not visible in the original photograph and so some enterprising printer has inserted a small picture of her in the leading car.

Cam Peak & Long Down from Dursley

A VIEW FROM STINCHCOMBE HILL across to Cam Peak and Long Down. Rosebery Terrace can be seen in the fields, as it was built for the work people of Listers in 1901.

MR. ROBINSON OUTSIDE HIS SHOP IN SILVER STREET, DURSLEY. Around him hang his wares, all of which 'the boy' would have had to put out each morning and take in at night. 'Bluebag Robinsons' was a popular store for many years. Before becoming a hardware shop it was two smaller premises – a grocer's and a candlemaker's.

LOOKING UP UNION STREET, DURSLEY, FROM CROSS BOULTON. The Union Workhouse that gave it its name, built in the 1830s, was at the top of the street on the right. Walters was a well-known bakery in the Market Place. The big building on the left housed Trull's shop which sold sweets and general goods.

UNION STREET, DURSLEY. Trull's house stands out at Cross Boulton and beyond at the bottom of the street are the chimneys of Elvey's brewery.

DURSLEY, C. 1909. A view from the tower of St James's Church towards Woodmancote. The tall terrace, centre, flanking Bull Pitch, is on the site of Vizards brewery, active in Victorian times.

THE BROADWELL TAVERN, DURSLEY, which sold Godsells fine ales. This area by the Broadwell pool is possibly the oldest part of the town. The tavern is an ancient building of unknown age, with a strange assortment of windows. It is said to have once been a monastic dwelling.

DURSLEY FROM STINCHCOMBE HILL. Left of centre in the foreground is the Tabernacle church and behind that the buildings of Castle Farm, the Methodist (later County) school and the Methodist chapel. The main entrance to the farm was opposite Parsonage Place, where the doctors have their surgeries, and it was common for traffic to have to cope with a herd of cattle ambling along Parsonage Street. Comparison with a modern picture shows the extent to which the town was ravaged by demolition in the 1950s and 1960s.

LONG STREET, DURSLEY, once the principal highway of the town linking the woolcloth mills on the stream at Townsend with the agricultural and business centre at the Market Place. It was in this street, from ancient times, that the wealthy had their houses.

THE PRIORY, DURSLEY. By tradition the Priory was built in the 1500s by a family called Webb hailing from the Low Countries. Like others, with names like Clutterbuck and Malpass, they had been invited to England to help improve the nation's wool cloth trade. It is said that in the late 1700s a local cardmaker would stand on the steps of the Priory and read aloud from the *Gloucester Journal* to any workers from the cloth mills who would listen. Newspapers then were a luxury for the well-to-do who could read.

DURSLEY MARKET PLACE, *c.* 1957. The building behind the 'no waiting' sign was built about 1840 as a branch of the National Provincial Bank, and later became the town's main post office. Beyond it is the police station built 1865. Soon after this photograph was taken, both buildings were demolished to allow traffic to go round the left hand side of the Town Hall.

THE MARKET PLACE, FROM PARSONAGE STREET. The shop on the right is Bailey's newsagents.

PARSONAGE STREET, LOOKING TOWARDS THE TOWN HALL, c. 1900. Thorley's Food is being advertised by H.R. Smith, whose chemist's shop was to the right of the horseless cart. This later became Boots. The high sign beyond advertises Eastmans Ltd.

SMITH & CHENEY'S DELIVERY CART. Early in this century chemists H.R. Smith became Smith & Cheney in the same premises. This cart, which looks new, was almost certainly used to deliver the mineral waters they made.

DR AND MRS BREWIS AT THEIR HOUSE AND SURGERY IN PARSONAGE STREET. In the 1870s the premises had belonged to an ironmonger, W.T. Tilton. He built the hall at the back (now the doctors' waiting-room) for use as a Mechanic's Institute.

PARSONAGE STREET, C. 1956. On the left is the new main post office for Dursley and, next to it, the end-of-terrace building used for many years as a telephone exchange, This was demolished later in a second attempt to ease the town's traffic problem.

A LEAFY LANE BELIEVED TO BE WHAT IS NOW REDNOCK DRIVE, C. 1914. The drive was originally a track for horse-drawn vehicles carrying wool and cloth to and from Dursley Lower Mill in the valley below, roughly half way between Upper Cam and Long Street. When Captain Graham bought the Rednock estate he closed the drive, making it a private road to his house. By about 1912 Sir Ashton Lister had acquired the estate and he reopened the drive to public vehicles, thereby allowing house building to begin in the Knapp.

THE 'NARROW WAY' TO STINCHCOMBE HILL FROM DURSLEY, which leaves Hill Road where it bends sharply left and becomes the Broadway. It emerges on the hilltop close to the golf club buildings.

STINCHCOMBE HILL FROM THE SOUTH. Most obvious is the absence of vegetation, kept away by the grazing of rabbits and sheep.

THE FOREST OF DEAN AND RIVER SEVERN, FROM STINCHCOMBE HILL. Part way along the road snaking its way towards the river is the hamlet known at The Quarry where the remains of stone extraction are still very obvious. Right foreground is the Yew Tree Inn built right up against the boundary with Stinchcombe parish, designated 'dry' by its Victorian incumbent the Revd Sir Charles Prevost.

THE RAILWAY BRIDGE AT UPPER CAM, c. 1955.

SOME OF THE WISE FAMILY AT LITTLECOMBE HOUSE, UPPER CAM. This stood just below Cam Meeting Chapel and behind can be seen part of The Quagg, and horses grazing in the hillside fields behind Kingshill House.

UPPER CAM, at the junction of Church Road, Hopton Road and Springhill.

CAM LONG DOWN, showing the old road that led to the quarry on top at the far end. Like Cam Peak, the Down is an outlier of the Cotswold Hills which once stretched much further westwards than now. As they receeded under the action of erosion, hills like the Peak, Long Down and Downham Hill have been left behind.

TEETOTAL COTTAGES, at Noggins Hole, Hopton Road, Cam. The cottages were so called because a tippler in the last century turned teetotal and saved so much money that he was able to build these and another rank closer to Upper Cam.

CAM HOPTON SCHOOL AND GREEN.

HOPTON ROAD, NEAR THE JUNCTION WITH UPTHORPE. The houses on the right were built with their backs to the road so that the Winterbotham family in their home up on Norman Hill across the valley could see the better front sides.

THE BOTTOM OF CAM PITCH, C. 1910. Behind the railings on the left can be seen a pump which was used by families on both sides of the road to get drinking water. In the days of steam lorries it was used for a different purpose, for these would stop here and fill up before chuffing up the hill.

COALEY, C. 1904. This type of rural scene seems idyllic now but behind the 'roses round the door' life was hard.

BERKELEY MARKET PLACE. Berkeley is an ancient settlement dating back to at least Saxon times when it had a coinage mint. Legends abound, including those of the witch who, after a great struggle, was carried off by the devil, and of the monstrous toad that was fed on the castle prisoners.

CHURCH HOUSE, SLIMBRIDGE, once the parish workhouse.

CHILDREN OF SLIMBRIDGE PAROCHIAL SCHOOL, which existed until 1906 next to the old workhouse. Miss Pick, headmistress during latter Victorian times, is seen here left, back row. The other teacher is thought to be Miss Malpass.

SHEPHERD'S PATCH, on the banks of the canal at Slimbridge. On the right is the Tudor Arms and on the left, the Patch Hotel. The baker's cart in the middle distance is probably Pearce's from Churchend, Slimbridge.

LOOKING NORTH TOWARDS CAMBRIDGE, 1911. On the left is the old police station where Mr Marsh would have been in charge. All the houses in the middle of this scene have been demolished. On the right is the house of Mr White, builder and decorator, and at the end of this a donkey-driven cider press, only recently dismantled.

CAMBRIDGE, looking northwards to the point where the old Dursley road came round the back of the school on the right. The school closed in 1906 and in turn was used as a store and then a meeting place for the British Legion. The finger-post, outside Cambridge Mill, curiously is marked 'Birmingham'. The row of cottages on the left were mill-workers' dwellings with Gladstone Cottage in the foreground. The fence and stabling on the right border the grounds of Cambridge House.

BERKELEY HUNT MEETING OUTSIDE THE WHITE LION INN, CAMBRIDGE, 1911. The White Lion was at one time a very busy hostelry with stabling for 12 to 14 horses. It is recorded that in the great days of the wool cloth trade teazles grown at Alveston would be carted to the mills of the Stroud valley, the carter stopping at the White Lion on his journeys.

JACK MOSS ON THE BACK OF A GLOUCESTER OLD SPOT PIG, C. 1917. At the time Jack's father, Daniel, was owner of the White Lion, Cambridge, and income from the drinks trade was augmented by breeding pigs and selling the meat locally.

A VIEW OF CAMBRIDGE FROM THE OLD DURSLEY ROAD, 1909. On the left is the village school erected in 1862 with endowment by Samuel Hadley, timber merchant and farmer of Cambridge Mill, off to the right of the picture.

CAMBRIDGE. Florence Hobbs, Maud Tudor and their children stand outside Bell Cottages.

SLYMBRIDGE STREET was the old name for Ryalls Lane, Cambridge. c. 1907. The men are standing at the junction of the lane with the A38.

ROLLS COURT, CAMBRIDGE, c. 1921, home then of the Peake family. Here Edward stands by the pony's head and with him are his children, Clara, Henry, Ernest and Kate. The land at the Court was farmed mainly as a dairy unit. The girls ran the house and farm and looked after numerous ducks and hens. The family also owned and operated Cambridge Mill, formerly a grain and woollen mill and of some antiquity. By 1830 it was a sawmill. At haymaking time mill-hands and timber-waggon horses would be called into service at Rolls Court.

HOPE HOUSE COTTAGES, RYALLS LANE, at the junction with Troy Town, also known as Tray or Trey Town. The name possibly indicates the third part of the parish,, the other two parts being Slimbridge and Cambridge. It was subject to severe flooding.

FLOODING AROUND THE GEORGE INN, CAMBRIDGE, c. 1925. Large-scale drainage schemes in recent years have alleviated this once regular problem.

THE GEORGE INN, CAMBRIDGE, looking south over the bridge to the village. It is said that the barn on the left of the picture was used as a pin factory.

THE DROVER'S ARMS INN, north of Cambridge.

THE FOX AND GOOSE INN, HALMORE. When R.S.M. William Workman was released from the army at the end of World War I he became publican of the Fox and Goose Inn, and is seen here with three of his daughters. In time, four of his daughters became teachers and all taught at Berkeley School.

JOSEPH STURGE AND HIS FAMILY AT PLANTATION HOUSE, SHARPNESS. The house had been built as a fishing lodge for the Berkeley family, but became home for the managers of Sharpness Pleasure Gardens.

A THATCHED COTTAGE IN SANIGAR LANE NEAR SHARPNESS.

PHOTOGRAPH CREDITS

N. Attwood • L. Ayliffe • M. Bailey • P.Bailey • Mrs Baker • Mrs M. Baker
Mrs A. Baldwin • M. Ball • Mrs M. Bartlett • G. Barton • Miss M. Barton • Mr Bird
G. Blandford • Miss E. Bloodworth • S. Bloodworth • M. Brace • R. Brown
E. Buston • Mrs B. Cale • C. Chandler • Revd E. Charlesworth • Mrs A. Collard
P. Collard • Mrs Coombe • Mrs D. Cross • Mrs J. Cullimore • A. Davies
Mrs J. Davis • K. Davis • W. Deacon • R. Denning • N. Downer • Mrs A. Dunlevy
Mrs S. Evans • A. Ford • Mr & Mrs D. Goodrich • Mrs R. Haines • Mrs D. Hall
K. Hall • I. Harris • R. Heathman • Mrs M. Henderson • Mrs A.E. Hill • C. Howarth
Mrs Jennings • Mrs K. Jones • Miss K. Kemp • Mrs G. Kilminster
Miss J. Kingham • Mr & Mrs W.P. Lawrence • Miss M. Miles • Mr & Mrs W. Mills
Mrs Morgan • J. Morris • J. Moss • P. Neale • F. Newman • W. Noad
Mrs D. Oldridge • Mrs Osborne • M. Owen • J. & J. Pallister • Miss Palser
Mrs Peacy • W. Peake • Mr Pegler • Mrs V. Pegler • Mrs E. Phillips
Mrs G. Poulter • Mr & Mrs C. Pyle • Mrs I. Richards • Mrs M. Sambell
Mrs D. Seeley • Mrs Shepherd • C. Smetham • G. Smith • Mrs P. Smith
B. Snow • Mrs P. Snow • S. Spencer • A. Sutton • Mrs E. Talboys • Miss V. Taylor
C. Timbrell • Mrs J. Tipper • Mrs L. Trollope • A. Tudor • Mrs M. Tudor
K. Vigus • L. Vaisey • Miss R. Wareham • M. Welsh • D. White • Mrs W. White
Miss A. Wintle • Mrs Wiseman